CONTENTS

W9-BPJ-589

Any words appearing in the text in bold, **like this,** are explained in the glossary. You can also look out for them in the word bank at the bottom of each page.

GLITTERING CRYSTALS

Crystals are the shapes that **minerals** form when they grow. Crystals come in all shapes and sizes, and are found in rocks all over the world. Some crystals can be as large as a house, while others are so tiny you can only see them under a powerful microscope.

Some crystals are very common, such as the crystals of salt in the salt shaker in your kitchen. Other crystals can be as rare and beautiful as diamonds.

Giant crystal

The largest crystal in the world is a crystal of a mineral called beryl. The crystal can be found in Madagascar. It is 60 feet (18 meters) long, 11 feet (3.5 meters) wide and weighs approximately 837,900 pounds (380,000 kilograms). Such large crystals are very rare. They only form in places that remain undisturbed for thousands of years.

mineral   naturally occurring particle. Rocks are made from lots of minerals.

Geology Rocks!

Crystals

Rebecca Faulkner

Raintree

Chicago, Illinois

Design: Victoria Bevan
and AMR Design Ltd (www.amrdesign.com)
Illustrations: David Woodroffe
Picture Research: Melissa Allison
Production: Duncan Gilbert

Originated by Chroma Graphics Pte. Ltd
Printed and bound in China by
South China Printing Company

11 10 09 08 07
10 9 8 7 6 5 4 3 2 1

**Library of Congress Cataloging-in-Publication
Data:**

Faulkner, Rebecca.
  Crystals / Rebecca Faulkner.
    p. cm. -- (Geology rocks!)
  Includes bibliographical references and index.
  ISBN-13: 978-1-4109-2751-4 (library binding -
hardcover)
  ISBN-10: 1-4109-2751-2 (library binding -
hardcover)
  ISBN-13: 978-1-4109-2759-0 (pbk.)
  ISBN-10: 1-4109-2759-8 (pbk.)
 1. Crystals--Juvenile literature. 2. Rocks--Analysis--
Juvenile
literature. I. Title.
  QD906.3.F39 2007
  548--dc22
                    2006037064

Acknowledgments
The publishers would like to thank the following
for permission to reproduce photographs:

Alamy p. **25** (Arco Images), pp. **5 top inset, 42**
(BE&W), p. **16** (Cassida Images), p. **40** (Doug Steley),
p. **31 inset** (Kike Calvo/VWPICS), p. **27 top** (Kirk
Treakle), pp. **5 bottom inset, 8** (Phototake Inc.),
p. **29 top** (Roger Cracknell), p. **34** (Scenics &
Science); Bridgeman Art Library p. **41** (Smithsonian
Institution, Washington DC, USA); Corbis pp. **6, 18,
31, 33, 36 amethyst, 36 clear**, p. **7** (Jose Manuel
Sanchis Calvete), p. **43** (Alison Wright); Gavin
Newman p. **4-5**; GeoScience Features Picture Library
pp. **12 quartz, 13, 24, 29 bottom, 35, 36 milky,
36 rose, 36 smoky, 38, 39**, p. **12 feldspar** (Prof.
B. Booth), pp. 12 **hornblende, 12 mica** (Visual
Unlimited); Harcourt Education Ltd. pp. **19, 22-23**
(Tudor Photography); Photolibrary.com p. **32**; Science
Photo Library p. **11** (Charles D. Winters), p. **17**
(Colin Cuthbert), p. **44** (Dirk Wiersma), p. **20** (Martin
Bond), p. **37** (Martin Land), p. **9 bottom** TIPS p.
28 (Guido Alberto Rossi); Visuals Unlimited pp. **12
centre, 27 bottom** (Doug Sokell), p. **26** (Dr. Ken
Wagner), p. **30** (Dr. Marli Miller), pp. **14, 21** (Mark A.
Schneider)

Cover photograph of quartz reproduced with
permission of Science Photo Library (Simon Fraser).

Every effort has been made to contact copyright
holders of any material reproduced in this book.
Any omissions will be rectified in subsequent
printings if notice is given to the publishers.

Disclaimer
All the Internet addresses (URLs) given in this book
were valid at the time of going to press. However,
due to the dynamic nature of the Internet, some
addresses may have changed, or sites may have
changed or ceased to exist since publication. While
the author and publishers regret any inconvenience
this may cause readers, no responsibility for any
such changes can be accepted by either the author
or the publishers.

We can see crystals all around us—in mountain ranges, on the beach, in riverbeds, in cliffs, and even in jewelry stores. Some crystals can take on amazing forms, and some sparkle in the light. Some crystals even glow in the dark. Crystals of fluorite glow bright blue or green in ultraviolet light. The largest crystal of fluorite ever found was discovered in New Mexico. It weighed more than 35 pounds (16 kilograms).

The diamonds, rubies, and sapphires you see in necklaces, bracelets, and rings are all examples of beautiful crystals. These take millions of years to form and are very rare, which is why they are so expensive. Most crystals form more quickly, over thousands of years, and are much smaller.

Find out later...

Why do dentists use diamonds?

How do crystals keep time?

Which crystal do we eat?

⬆ **Lechuguilla Cave, in New Mexico, is 120 miles (193 kilometers) long and 1,641 feet (500 meters) deep. It contains whole chambers filled with amazing gypsum and aragonite crystals, including some more than 20 feet (6 meters) long.**

WHAT ARE CRYSTALS?

Naming crystals

The word "crystal" comes from the Greek word *krystallos*, which means "ice." The Greeks found beautiful quartz crystals in the Alps mountains and believed that they were a form of water frozen so hard that they would never thaw.

The **minerals** that make up rocks are usually **crystalline**, which means they are made of crystals joined together. The crystals occur naturally and are solid substances made up of tiny particles called **atoms**.

Most crystals contain two or more types of atom. Crystals of gypsum are made from calcium, oxygen, and sulphur atoms. The salt crystals you add to your food are made from sodium and chlorine atoms. Only some crystals are made from just one type of atom. Crystals of the mineral gold contain only gold atoms, and diamond crystals contain only carbon atoms.

⇨ Rocks are made of minerals that come in a variety of colors, sizes, and shapes.

atom tiny particle that elements and minerals are made from
crystalline made of crystals joined together

The atoms in crystals are arranged in three-dimensional patterns called **lattices**. These lattices have regular geometric shapes such as hexagons or pyramids. As a crystal grows this lattice will repeat itself in all directions. Because of this, if a crystal can grow freely it will have a regular geometric shape.

Each crystal of a particular mineral contains the same type of atom arranged in the same way, and so each crystal will have the same shape. A diamond, for example, will always be made from carbon atoms, and its atoms will always be arranged in the same way. Quartz crystals always contain silicon and oxygen atoms, and always grow as six-sided columns.

Flat faces

Because crystals form geometric shapes they have flat faces called **crystal faces**. The angle between these faces is always the same for crystals of the same mineral.

⬇ **These crystals of galena have a crystal lattice, which means they grow in regular cube shapes.**

lattice three dimensional pattern or framework

Which crystals do you know?

Crystals are very important in our daily lives. Many of the things you use every day are made from crystals. Your watch, your computer, and even your toothpaste all have parts made from crystals.

Crystals can be found all over your home. In the kitchen you will find crystals of halite in your salt shaker. Halite is rock salt. If you add salt to your food at mealtimes you are actually adding crystals of halite to your food. The glass that you drink from and the mirror that you look at yourself in are made from crystals of quartz. The knives and forks that you use to eat your dinner contain crystals of chromite. The detergent that goes in the washing machine to wash your clothes is often made from borax crystals.

Crystals in toothpaste

Did you know that the toothpaste you use to clean your teeth is made of tiny crystals of many different **minerals**? When you wake up in the morning and brush your teeth you are using crystals of fluorite, calcite, and quartz.

You add these crystals to your food. They are crystals of halite seen under a microscope. You can see that each crystal is almost a perfect cube.

piezoelectricity ability to vibrate at a certain speed when an electric current is passed through

Your watch uses quartz crystals to keep time. Quartz crystals have a property called **piezoelectricity**. This means a crystal vibrates at a certain speed when an electric current is passed through it. The vibration of the crystal keeps time in your watch. The silica from quartz is also used to make silicon chips that power computers.

The paint that you use in your art class may get its color from crystals. Because many of them are bright colors, crystals can be ground into powder and made into paint. When you use a pencil you are writing with crystals of graphite.

Hard and soft

Crystals of corundum are very hard, so they are used to make emery boards for filing nails. Crystals of talc are very soft, so they are used for talcum powder and baby powder.

Without microchips computers would not work. Microchips are made from quartz crystals.

Did you know that a quartz watch actually uses crystals of quartz to keep the time?

CRYSTALS ALL OVER EARTH

We can see crystals in the rocks all around us. They can be high in mountain ranges, or hidden in sand grains on the beach. Some crystals can take on amazing forms. Some are large and beautiful such as diamonds and rubies. These are called **gemstones**.

Most crystals form deep inside Earth as hot liquid rock called **magma** cools and hardens. As the magma hardens crystals form, so we say it **crystallizes** into rock.

If we could dig deep into Earth we would see that the inside is like an onion. It is made up of different layers.

Tiny crystals everywhere

The rocks of Earth's crust are made from crystals. We cannot always see these crystals because many of them are too small to be seen with the naked eye, but they are definitely there.

mantle

outer core

inner core

crust

⇨ The outer layer of Earth is called the crust. It is made of different types of rock.

crystallization cooling and hardening of magma to form igneous rock
magma molten rock from the mantle

The **crust** is like the skin of the onion. It is a relatively thin layer covering the surface of Earth. There are two types of crust: continental and oceanic. Continental crust is found beneath the continents and can be up to 45 miles (70 kilometers) thick. Oceanic crust is found beneath the oceans and is up to 6 miles (10 kilometers) thick. It is heavier than continental crust.

If we could peel away the crust we would find the **mantle**. This is a thick layer that starts at the base of the crust and extends 1,800 miles (2,900 kilometers) deep into Earth. This is where magma crystallizes into rock.

If you could travel deep down into the center of Earth you would find the **core**. The core can be separated into the outer core (which is liquid) and the inner core (which is solid).

Melting rock

The rocks in the mantle are so hot—up to 5,500° Fahrenheit (3,000° Celsius)—that they are partly **molten**. Crystals of a **mineral** called olivine are common in the upper mantle, but olivine is much rarer in the crust. It is only found where molten material from the mantle reaches the surface of Earth's crust, for example in volcanoes.

⬆ Large green crystals of olivine form in the mantle. It is very rare to find them on Earth's surface.

Rock types

Earth's **crust** is made up of three types of rock:
- **igneous rocks**
- **sedimentary rocks**
- **metamorphic rocks**.

Igneous rocks are formed from **magma**. Over millions of years the magma rises up from the **mantle** and through Earth's crust. As it does so, it cools and crystallizes to form igneous rock. This usually happens underground, but it can happen at Earth's surface when magma is ejected from volcanoes.

Many sedimentary rocks are formed from broken bits of other rocks. When igneous rocks are attacked by wind and rain, tiny particles of rock and **minerals** are broken off and carried away. These minerals are eventually deposited in a new place and build up over millions of years to form new sedimentary rock.

Hard rocks

If a rock contains crystals of hard minerals, such as quartz, it will be a hard rock. The igneous rock **granite** contains lots of crystals of quartz so we know that it is hard.

quartz

feldspar

mica

hornblende

The igneous rock granite is made up of crystals of the minerals quartz, feldspar, mica, and hornblende.

granite hard igneous rock

Metamorphic rocks are formed when heat or high pressure changes igneous or sedimentary rocks. When hot magma rises below Earth's surface it heats up the surrounding rocks. When mountain ranges form on Earth the rocks buried below experience immense pressure. All this extra heat and pressure causes the minerals in the rocks to change (metamorphose) into other minerals.

As the crystals of different minerals grow they interlock and join together to create different types of rock. Different types of mineral crystals combine to make rocks in the same way as ingredients combine to make a salad. You can make a salad that contains a variety of ingredients, such as lettuce, cucumbers, and green peppers, or you can make a salad that consists only of lettuce.

In the same way, a rock may contain many different mineral crystals or may be made up of just one mineral. The igneous rock granite contains crystals of the minerals quartz, feldspar, mica, and hornblende. The metamorphic rock marble consists entirely of calcite crystals.

Rock forming minerals

There are more than 4,000 different minerals on Earth. Only about 100 of them are commonly found on Earth. These minerals can combine in many different ways to make rocks.

⬆ Large crystals of the mineral garnet are sometimes found in metamorphic rocks. These crystals are used in jewelry.

Crystals on the move

Most crystals form deep inside Earth, but they appear at the surface of Earth in some places where the soil and rocks above have been eroded away.

On Earth there is an unending cycle of rock formation, break down (**weathering**), transportation (**erosion**), and settlement in a new place (**deposition**). All these processes make up what is called the **rock cycle**.

The surface of Earth may seem solid but, eventually, even the hardest rocks are worn away as they are attacked by the wind and rain. This is called weathering and, over millions of years, pieces of rock are chipped away and broken down into clumps of the crystals that created them.

Heavy rains

In Brazil and Sri Lanka many beautiful crystals of topaz, ruby, diamond, emerald, garnet, and tourmaline are left behind in piles of weathered rock after heavy rains.

⬇ Stunning crystals of topaz, as large as car headlights, have been found in Russia and Brazil.

deposition laying down weathered rock in a new place

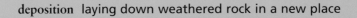

These broken pieces of crystal are small enough to be carried away to different places by wind, rivers, or ice. This is called erosion.

Hard crystals are able to withstand the forces of weathering and erosion. Many valuable crystals, such as diamonds, rubies, and sapphires, are very hard. When they are eroded from rocks they are not destroyed, but can end up traveling long distances in rivers. Some may be dumped at the edge of a river during a flood, and others will travel all the way to the ocean.

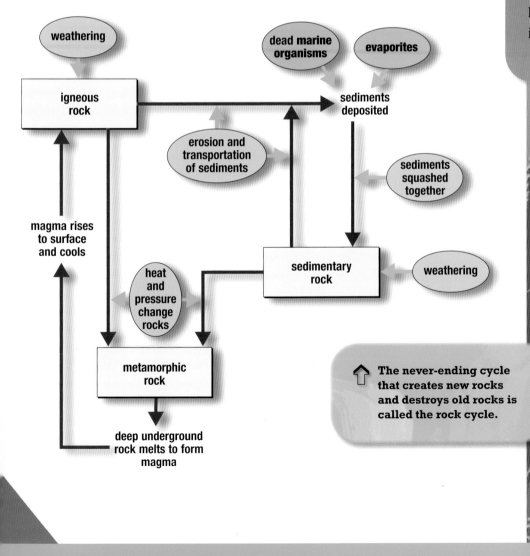

weathering

dead **marine** organisms

evaporites

igneous rock

sediments deposited

erosion and transportation of sediments

sediments squashed together

magma rises to surface and cools

sedimentary rock

weathering

heat and pressure change rocks

metamorphic rock

deep underground rock melts to form magma

⬆ The never-ending cycle that creates new rocks and destroys old rocks is called the rock cycle.

CRYSTALS UNDER THE MICROSCOPE

Studying crystals

The study of crystals is called **crystallography**, and scientists who study crystals are called crystallographers.

Many crystals are so small they can only be seen under a microscope.

Crystallographers can study the crystals in a rock sample by cutting very thin slices of the rock with a diamond saw. These are called **thin sections,** and they can be examined under a microscope. When the rocks are magnified in this way, we can see the individual crystals they contain. We can also see how the crystals fit together so tightly that there are no spaces between them.

We can see tiny crystals in rock by looking at a very thin slice of rock under a microscope. This can help us figure out what minerals are in a rock.

crystallographer scientist who studies crystals
crystallography the study of crystals

The microscope used by crystallographers to study crystals is called a petrological microscope. It has special filters that make the **minerals** appear brightly colored so the crystals are easy to see.

Sometimes the crystals are so tiny that they cannot be seen under the petrological microscope. In this case, crystallographers use very powerful microscopes called electron microscopes.

Micrographs and magnification

A photograph taken through a microscope is called a **micrograph**. Micrographs show the individual crystals of the minerals in rocks. The petrological microscope can magnify crystals up to 2,000 times. The electron microscope can magnify crystals up to 1,000,000 times.

 An electron microscope allows scientists to see amazing detail in crystals.

micrograph   photograph taken through a microscope
thin section   very thin slice of rock mounted on a microscope slide

What's inside a crystal?

Atomic structure
By shining X-rays through crystals scientists can see how the atoms inside the crystal are packed together. This is called the **atomic structure** of the crystal.

How do we know that the **atoms** inside a crystal are arranged in three-dimensional **lattices**? Scientists can see inside a crystal by shining a beam of X-rays through it, just as a doctor can see broken bones inside your body when an X-ray is taken.

There are many different ways that atoms can be arranged in crystals. They all form three-dimensional lattices. Some crystals are made of one type of atom. For example, diamond is made from only carbon atoms. Most crystals contain two or more types of atom.

The same atoms can **crystallize** into different patterns under different conditions. For example, when carbon crystals form under intense temperature and pressure deep inside Earth, they can form diamond. If the crystals form nearer the surface of Earth's **crust,** the carbon can take the form of graphite.

The atoms in a crystal are stacked in an orderly way, just like these tomatoes.

The carbon atoms in graphite are arranged in layers of hexagonal patterns. The layers can slide across each other, so this explains why graphite is soft and splits easily. The atoms in diamond are tightly packed in a strong lattice made up of pyramid shapes called tetrahedra. This explains why diamond is so hard.

Diamond (right) and graphite (left) are examples of polymorphs. They both consist of carbon atoms, but the atoms are arranged differently to form the different crystals.

Polymorphism

Graphite and diamond are **polymorphs** of carbon. This means they contain the same atoms, but have different atomic structures. Polymorphism is very common.

Diamond:

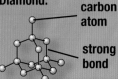

carbon atom

strong bond

Graphite:

atoms in one layer:

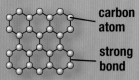

carbon atom

strong bond

a stack of layers:

weak bonds between layers

How Do I Look?

The shape of a crystal is determined by the way the **atoms** inside it are arranged. Crystals grow in strange and beautiful geometric shapes.

Crystal systems

Each **mineral** forms crystals with a characteristic shape. Depending on the atoms involved in making the crystals, different shapes may result. These crystal shapes can be divided into six categories called **crystal systems**.

Massive minerals

Sometimes minerals form in spaces where there is not enough room for crystals to grow. When there is just a big chunk of a mineral it is called a massive mineral.

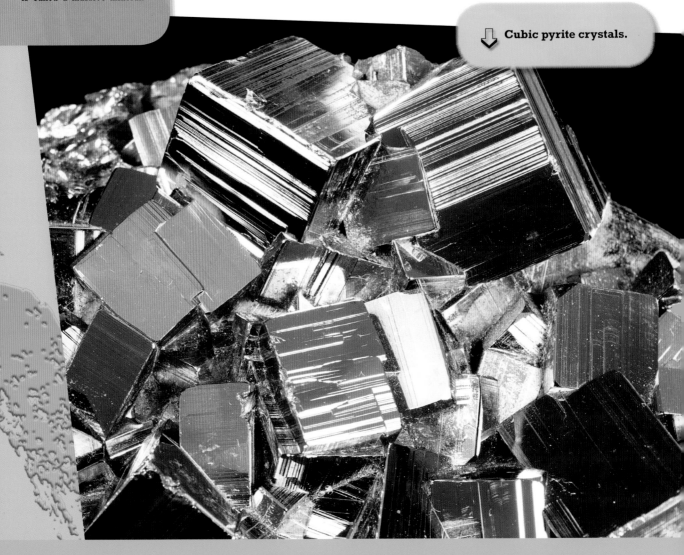

⬇ **Cubic pyrite crystals.**

cyrstal system one of six categories that crystals are divided into

Cubic crystals

Crystals of the cubic system are often, but not always, shaped like symmetrical cubes (blocks). There are many other crystal shapes in the cubic system, such as octahedrons (eight faces) and dodecahedrons (ten faces). Examples of minerals that form cubic crystals are pyrite, diamond, garnet, galena, and fluorite.

Tetragonal crystals

Tetragonal crystals are shaped like elongated four-sided prisms with pyramids at each end. This is one of the less common crystal systems, but examples include rutile, zircon, and cassiterite.

Salt crystals

If you look at salt under a microscope you will see that each tiny crystal is shaped like a cube. Halite crystals belong to the cubic system.

A tetragonal crystal of rutile.

Monoclinic system

Monoclinic is the most common **crystal system**. The crystals are short and stubby with tilted faces at each end. Examples of **minerals** that form monoclinic crystals include mica, gypsum, amphibole, orthoclase, and azurite.

Hexagonal/trigonal system

The hexagonal and trigonal systems are grouped together because they are very similar. Hexagonal crystals are shaped like six-sided prisms with pyramids at each end, while trigonal crystals are three-sided prisms. Crystals of apatite, beryl, calcite, quartz, and graphite all fall into this system.

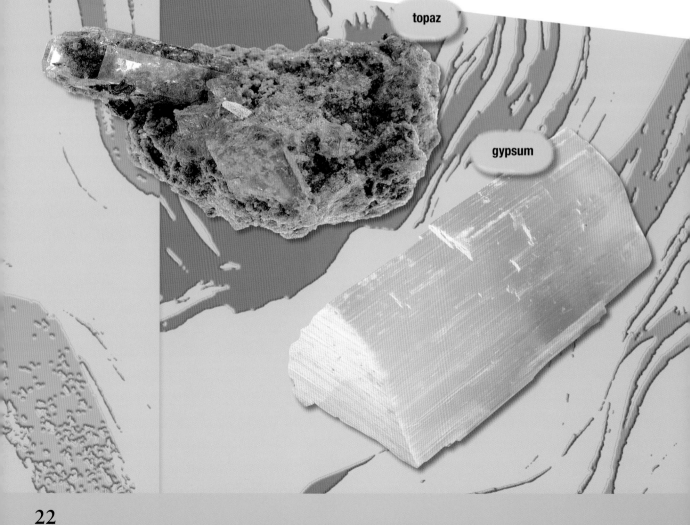

topaz

gypsum

Orthorhombic system

Crystals of the orthorhombic system are short and stubby prisms with pyramids at either end. They can look a little like matchboxes and are very common. Topaz, olivine, sulphur, and barite crystals are part of this system.

Triclinic system

Triclinic crystals are usually flat with sharp edges. The crystals are not normally symmetrical and can have strange shapes. This is the rarest crystal system and includes kaolinite and turquoise.

Thousands of possibilities

Calcite crystals can grow in more than 2,500 different shapes, more than for any other mineral. All calcite crystals belong to the trigonal system and have the same arrangement of calcium, carbon, and oxygen **atoms**. What is the reason for these thousands of different shapes? Differences in temperature and pressure inside Earth cause the crystal faces to grow at different rates, which creates many different variations on one basic shape.

⬇ **Topaz has orthorhombic crystals, gypsum has monoclinic crystals, apatite has hexagonal crystals, and quartz has trigonal crystals.**

apatite

quartz

Crystal habit

The **crystal systems** refer to the way an individual crystal grows. However, crystals do not usually grow alone. More commonly many crystals grow together. The way crystals grow and interlock with each other is called the crystal **habit**.

Crystals of quartz and beryl often form prisms and so are said to have a prismatic habit. Crystals that have a thread-like appearance are called fibrous. The **minerals** serpentine and asbestos form fibrous crystals. Crystals that have a needle-like appearance, such as natrolite, are called acicular.

Blocks and tables

Crystals that look like building blocks are said to have a blocky habit. Orthoclase has a blocky habit. Crystals that are flat, like a table, have a tabular habit. Barite has a tabular habit.

⬆ This spiky mineral is called stibnite. It is made of acicular crystals that look like needles.

Malachite crystals often occur in mammilated or botryoidal forms. In mammilated minerals the crystals appear as rounded lumps. In botryoidal forms they look like a bunch of grapes, because each crystal grows outwards from its center.

Crystals such as copper, which grow in such a way that they resemble the branches of a tree, have a dendritic habit. We say crystals have a lamellar habit if they are flat sheets and look like the pages of a book. Muscovite mica crystals grow in this way.

⬇ **This crystal of hematite has what is called a reniform habit. The word renal means "to do with the kidneys," and you can see that the crystal is kidney shaped.**

Common crystal habits

These are some common crystal habits:

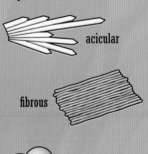

acicular

fibrous

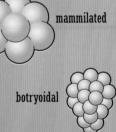

mammilated

botryoidal

How Do Crystals Grow?

Grow your own crystals

You can grow your own salt crystals at home, and see how they always form cubic shapes. There are many crystal-growing kits you can buy, or you can find a recipe for growing crystals on the Internet.

Crystals grow in a variety of ways and at different speeds to form very different shapes. Each crystal starts off very small and grows outward as more **atoms** are added. As a crystal grows, the regular geometric shape of the crystal **lattice** will repeat itself in all directions. Because of this, if a crystal can grow freely it will have a regular geometric shape.

In nature a huge variety of crystal shapes will form because crystals are rarely free to grow in all directions. They usually grow alongside other crystals and interlock with them to form a variety of different shapes. Different temperature and pressure conditions will also affect how atoms combine to produce endless crystal variations.

⬇ **Gypsum crystals form as water evaporates in desert areas.**

evaporate turn into a gas

Crystals are always forming, both at Earth's surface and deep inside Earth. There are two main ways that crystals grow.

Most crystals grow when liquid **magma** deep within Earth cools and hardens. As magma cools it changes from a liquid into solid crystals. Many crystals form at the same time. They crowd into one another and produce irregular shapes.

Other crystals form when water that contains dissolved **minerals,** called mineral-rich water, cools or **evaporates** leaving the minerals behind. The minerals then grow as crystals.

Crystals from gas

Crystals can even grow from gases that are rich in minerals. This happens in volcanic areas as hot gases cool when they reach the surface and deposit crystals. Sulphur crystals can form on the sides of volcanoes in this way.

⬇ Sulphur crystals can grow from volcanic gases on the sides of volcanoes.

➡ The crystals you can see in this granite rock formed deep inside Earth as magma cooled.

Growth in water

Crystals can form when hot water **evaporates** in volcanic areas or when salt water evaporates from lagoons, seas, and lakes in desert areas. As the water evaporates, any **minerals** in the water are left behind and form crystals.

The salt you add to your food forms in this way. The geologists' name for table salt is halite, and it forms cube-shaped crystals when water evaporates in desert areas.

Hot springs are common in volcanic areas because water is heated by the hot, rising **magma**. This hot water dissolves many minerals as it passes through the surrounding rocks. When this water reaches the surface and evaporates, calcite crystals often form near hot springs.

Halite crystals

Halite crystals are growing today around Salt Lake in Utah, and around the edge of the Dead Sea on the border between Israel and Jordan.

These are halite crystals that formed as water from an ancient lagoon evaporated.

stalactite thin icicle-shaped lump of rock that forms as water drips from cave ceilings

Calcite crystals form when water evaporates in limestone areas. Water passing through the limestone rocks picks up calcite. When this mineral-rich water drips into caves it can form spectacular deposits of calcite that look like icicles. These are called **stalactites** and **stalagmites**.

When water flows through hot rocks deep in the **crust** it dissolves minerals. If this mineral-rich water then flows towards the surface of the crust it will cool, and the minerals will crystallize. Crystals of gold, galena, and fluorite can form in this way.

Iceland spar

The largest calcite crystal in the world was found in Helgustadir in Iceland. It was a type of calcite called Iceland spar and it measured 23 feet (7 meters) long, 23 feet (7 meters) high, and 7 feet (2 meters) deep. It weighed more than 551,250 pounds (250,000 kilograms).

⬆ These amazing rocks are made of calcite crystals and are called travertine. They have formed over thousands of years as water from hot springs has evaporated.

➡ These gold crystals are formed as mineral-rich water rises towards Earth's surface and cools.

stalagmite short, stubby column of rock that forms when water drips onto a cave floor and evaporates

Growth in magma

Crystals are formed as hot liquid **magma** rises up from the **mantle** and travels towards the surface of Earth. As it does so, it cools and crystallizes, either underground or at Earth's surface—both on land and under water.

Crystallization is when the magma cools and hardens to form crystals. If magma cools slowly underground, there is plenty of time for crystals to form, and so the crystals can grow to large sizes. The rock produced in this way is made up of large crystals. We say it is **coarse grained**.

Crystals in granite

Granite is an example of a coarse grained rock. It contains crystals of the **minerals** quartz, feldspar, mica, and hornblende. When granite forms, as the magma cools underground, feldspar begins to crystallize first. For this reason feldspar crystals are often larger and more developed than the crystals of the other minerals.

⬇ This rock is called pegmatite. It formed when magma cooled slowly underground, so the crystals are large. Pegmatite often contains large crystals of **gemstones** such as topaz and beryl.

lava name for magma when it reaches the surface of Earth

When magma rises all the way to Earth's surface it is called **lava**. Sometimes this lava erupts onto the surface of the **crust** through volcanoes. Once on the surface, the lava cools quickly, so there is little time for crystals to develop before the rock hardens. As a result the crystals will be small. We say that rock containing small crystals is **fine grained**. Tiny crystals of feldspar, pyroxene, and olivine create rocks such as **basalt**.

Melting rocks

Molten magma is so hot that as it rises through the rocks of Earth's crust it can melt the surrounding rocks. This allows new crystals to grow. Some beautiful gemstone crystals are formed in this way, for example garnet.

⬆ **Large crystals of garnet can form deep inside Earth's crust.**

⬆ **Lava from erupting volcanoes cools rapidly at Earth's surface, which means there is little time for crystals to grow.**

The wonderful world of geodes

All of the rocks of Earth's **crust** are made up of crystals, but large well-defined crystals are rare.

The best places to find amazing crystals of rare **minerals** are in cavities in rocks where the crystals are able to grow freely. Amazing formations of minerals can be found in **geodes**. A geode looks like a normal rock, but it is hollow. When it is split open a lining of beautiful crystals is revealed.

Geode facts

The most common crystal found in geodes is quartz, in various colorful forms, especially amethyst and agate. Calcite can also be found. The largest geodes are big enough for you to crawl inside.

When the crystals have enough space to grow, amethyst crystals can fill the inside of a geode.

geode hollow rock lined with crystals

Geodes usually form in volcanic areas when **lava** cools. Lava often contains a lot of gas bubbles. Sometimes a gas bubble will become trapped as the lava solidifies into rock. This forms a cavity in the rock, which is an ideal site for crystals to form. When water passes through the lava it will dissolve some of the minerals. This mineral-rich water may become trapped in a cavity and deposit its minerals there. As the lava cools, the minerals crystallize inside the cavity. There is space around them, so the crystals can grow freely in all directions to produce large, spectacular crystals.

The rough exterior of the geode gives no clues about the secrets held inside it. The crystal lining of geodes is only revealed when the rock is split open.

Geodes and nodules

A geode that is completely filled with small, compact crystal formations such as agate is called a nodule. The only difference between a geode and a nodule is that a geode has a hollow cavity, whereas a nodule is solid.

The beautiful crystal lining of a nodule is revealed when it is split open.

ARE ALL CRYSTALS PERFECT?

Cross-shaped crystals

Staurolite crystals are named after the Greek word *stauros*, which means "cross," because they often grow through one another to form cross-shaped crystals.

Crystals rarely have perfect shapes. **Minerals** can only grow into perfect crystal shapes if they have enough space when they are growing. Most of the time there are so many different crystals growing in the same area that they all compete for space, and none of the crystals can grow very large.

Growing crystals are extremely sensitive to even minor changes in their environment. Slight changes in the temperature or pressure, or the addition of even a tiny speck of dust, can produce strange and wonderful crystals.

⇨ You can see how these twinned crystals of staurolite have grown through one another.

Crystals within crystals

Crystals often grow in strange ways. They may look like they are stuck together, or one crystal may grow into or through another one to form amazing shapes. This is called **twinning**, and is common in feldspar, aragonite, and gypsum crystals.

Sometimes a crystal of one mineral will grow on top of a crystal of a different mineral. In most cases, you can still see the shape of the crystal underneath, even though it may have been completely covered by the overgrowing crystal.

In extreme cases a large crystal, for example quartz, may grow around a smaller crystal, such as a crystal of pyrite, so that the smaller crystal is completely enclosed within the larger crystal.

Needle-shaped crystals
Sometimes needle-shaped golden or red rutile crystals can form inside quartz crystals. This happens very rarely, but when it does it produces amazing crystals called maiden hair.

⬆ When rutile crystals form inside quartz crystals the result looks like hair, which is why they are called "maiden hair."

Crystal impurities

Impurities in quartz

- Black or brown smoky quartz forms when impurities of aluminium are present.
- White milky quartz forms when small cavities in the quartz are filled with liquids, such as water, that make it look white.
- Pink rose quartz forms where impurities of titanium are present.
- Purple amethyst forms when impurities of iron are present.

If a tiny piece of rock or **mineral** lands on a crystal as it is growing it may have a dramatic effect. When this happens the piece of rock or mineral is called an **impurity**. Pure quartz crystals are colorless, but if a tiny amount of iron, aluminium, or other impurity enters the crystal **lattice,** then a different colored quartz will be produced.

The blue color of sapphires and red color of rubies are caused by impurities in the crystals. Both ruby and sapphire crystals form in the mineral corundum. If impurities of chromium are present then bright red rubies will form. If impurities of iron and titanium enter the crystal lattice, then blue sapphires will form.

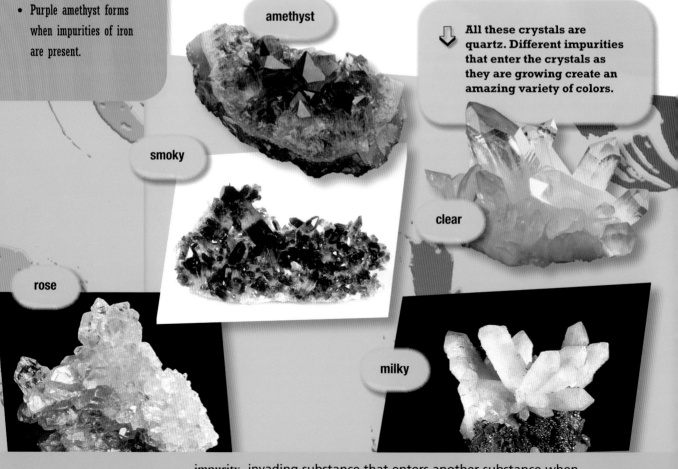

amethyst

All these crystals are quartz. Different impurities that enter the crystals as they are growing create an amazing variety of colors.

smoky

clear

rose

milky

impurity invading substance that enters another substance when it is growing

Sometimes you can only see the effects of impurities if you look at a crystal under a microscope. It is very rare to find a perfectly clear diamond because most contain tiny amounts of impurities that you can only see under a microscope.

Grains of sand often get in the way of growing gypsum crystals in deserts. When this happens, the crystal grows around the sand grains and encloses them as impurities in the crystal. This type of growth is called desert rose gypsum because the crystals are flat and look like rose petals.

The Hope diamond

A deep-blue diamond known as the Hope Diamond was found in India. This unusual color comes from impurities of boron that have entered the crystal lattice.

In deserts, gypsum can occur as desert rose, a flower-like form with embedded sand grains.

HOW DO CRYSTALS BREAK UP?

If you were to hit a lump of rock with a hammer, the crystals within the rock would break along internal lines of weakness called **cleavage planes**. Crystals of the same **mineral** will always break in the same way. In other words they will always have the same cleavage.

Some crystals break in only one direction. Others break in two or more directions. When cleavage planes are in one direction, the crystal tends to break into flat sheets, for example muscovite mica. Where there are two cleavage planes, the crystals breaks into elongated fragments, for example pyroxene. When there are three or more cleavage planes, the crystals may break into almost perfect cubic fragments, for example galena and halite.

Cleavage planes

one cleavage plane

two cleavage planes

three cleavage planes

Minerals can break into sheets, elongated fragments, or cubes depending on how many cleavage planes there are.

In this cubic crystal of galena there are three cleavages parallel to the cube faces.

cleavage plane line of weakness in a mineral, along which the mineral tends to break

Some crystals, for example quartz, have no cleavage planes, so they break or fracture in any direction and form a variety of shapes. If you were to hit a sample of quartz with a hammer it would fracture like a pane of glass.

⬆ **Mica crystals have one cleavage plane, so they break into sheets.**

Cutting crystals

When crystals are cut for use in jewelry, they are cut along the cleavage planes. If a crystal is cut across a cleavage plane this may cause the crystal to shatter. This is an expensive mistake if the crystal being cut is a valuable **gemstone**!

HOW DO WE USE CRYSTALS?

You use crystals every day, and they have many uses. One of the most common ways in which crystals have been used is in jewelry.

Gemstones in jewelry

Diamonds, rubies, sapphires, and garnets are called **gemstones** and have been used in jewelry for thousands of years. They are highly valued because of their beauty and rarity. Large, richly colored crystals can occasionally form, and these are worth a lot of money. The different colors are caused by **impurities** in the **minerals**.

The most valuable gemstones—the precious gemstones—are those that are the rarest, hardest, and most beautiful. They include diamonds, rubies, emeralds, and sapphires. The crystals are cut and polished in special ways so that light reflects off the surface and the crystal sparkles.

Gemstone qualities

A gemstone has three qualities that separate it from other crystals: rarity, beauty, and durability. Rarity and beauty increase its value. Durability (hardness) ensures the gemstone will last a long time.

➡ How would you feel if you found a lump of rock with amazing sapphire crystals like this?

Diamonds are the most valuable of all gemstones. They are very rare. Diamond is the hardest and most transparent mineral known. Light can pass through it, and this is what makes a diamond sparkle so brightly. Most diamonds are colorless, but impurities can make them any color of the rainbow.

Other crystal gemstones are called semi-precious gemstones, and these are not as expensive. They include garnet, tourmaline, amethyst, and topaz. Garnet can be blood-red in color. Tourmaline, topaz, and amethyst can be found in a huge variety of colors. Colorless topaz crystals are often mistaken for diamond crystals.

Powerful gemstones?
Some gemstones are believed to have special powers. The ancient Egyptians made amulets (necklaces) encrusted with gemstones to protect them from harm. The ancient Chinese believed that jade would protect their bodies from decay and allow them to live forever.

⬅ Most diamonds you see in jewelry appear colorless, but occasionally they can have amazing colors, like the blue in the Hope Diamond shown here. This is due to impurities in the crystal **lattice**.

Planes, paint, and plaster

Because gemstones are so rare and expensive, and take millions of years to form, **crystallographers** have learned how to make some crystals artificially. These artificial crystals are called **synthetic crystals**.

As well as being used for jewelry, crystals are used in many other ways. Most of the diamonds found on Earth are too small or shaped too strangely to be used in jewelry. Because the carbon **atoms** that make up diamond are so tightly packed, diamond crystals are very hard. This means they are ideal for use in cutting tools and drills.

Before refrigerators were invented, crystals of halite (rock salt) were used to preserve food. Halite is still used as a preservative today, as well as to flavor food.

Artificial gems

Synthetic diamonds can be made using cubic zirconia crystals. Synthetic emeralds, rubies, and sapphires can also be made for use in jewelry. Some of these synthetic gemstones are made so well it is very difficult to tell that they are not real.

⬆ Crystals of emerald can be grown artificially for use in jewelry.

⬇ The drill a dentist uses is made from diamond.

Corundum crystals are the second-hardest crystals known. The only harder substance is diamond. Corundum crystals and industrial-grade diamonds are used to grind and polish gemstones.

Crystals of rutile are an important source of titanium. This is used to make airplanes because it is very light. It is also used to make white paint.

Crystals of quartz are used in watches because they keep time. The silica in quartz is also used to make glass windowpanes, lenses for glasses, and silicon chips that are used in many electronic items, from space shuttles to coffee makers, traffic lights, and computers. Scientists can make synthetic crystals of quartz for all of these uses.

⬆ Halite is mined and piled up in huge salt mountains where it is left to dry out.

CONCLUSION

Crystals occur naturally and are solid substances made up of **atoms** arranged in three-dimensional **lattices**. They come in all shapes and sizes and are found in rocks all over Earth. The shape of a crystal is determined by the way that the atoms inside it are arranged. Some crystals can take on amazing forms. Some form large, beautiful crystals such as diamonds and rubies.

Crystals are always forming, both at the surface and deep inside Earth. They can either form inside Earth when hot liquid material called **magma crystallizes** into rock, or when mineral-rich water **evaporates** at Earth's surface.

Crystals are very important to us in our daily lives. You can find them in your watch, your computer, and even your toothpaste. Rare and beautiful crystals have been used in jewelry for thousands of years.

⇨ **Tourmaline crystals are often very colorful. This one has colors like a watermelon.**

FIND OUT MORE

Books

Dunlop, Jenna. *Minerals*. New York: Crabtree, 2004.

Farndon, John. *Rocks and Minerals*. New York: DK, 2005.

Graham, Ian. *Earth's Precious Resources: Minerals*. Chicago: Heinemann Library, 2005.

Using the Internet

Explore the Internet to find out more about crystals. You can use a search engine, such as www.yahooligans.com, and type in keywords such as:
• geode
• crystallography
• diamond

Websites

These websites are useful starting places for finding out more about geology:

Mineralogical Society of America: www.minsocam.org

How to Identify Minerals, San Diego Natural History Museum: www.sdnhm.org/kids/minerals/how-to.html

Rocks for Kids: www.rocksforkids.com

Search tips

There are billions of pages on the Internet so it can be difficult to find exactly what you are looking for. These search tips will help you find websites more quickly:
• Know exactly what you want to find out about first.
• Use two to six keywords in a search, putting the most important words first.
• Be precise. Only use names of people, places, or things.

GLOSSARY

atom tiny particle that elements and minerals are made from

atomic structure how the atoms inside a crystal are packed together

basalt fine-grained igneous rock

cleavage plane line of weakness in a mineral, along which the mineral tends to break

coarse grained large grains

core central layer of Earth

crust thin surface layer of Earth

crystal face flat side of a crystal

crystalline made of crystals joined together

crystallization cooling and hardening of magma to form igneous rock

crystallographer scientist who studies crystals

crystallography study of crystals

crystal system one of six categories that crystals are divided into

deposition laying down weathered rock in a new place

erosion removal and transportation of weathered rock

evaporate turn into a gas

evaporite sediment left behind as water evaporates

fine grained tiny grains

gemstone crystal that is cut and polished for use in jewelry

geode hollow rock lined with crystals

granite hard igneous rock

habit way crystals grow and interlock with each other

igneous rock rock formed from magma either underground or at Earth's surface

impurity invading substance that enters another substance when it is growing

lattice three dimensional pattern or framework

lava name for magma when it reaches the surface of Earth

magma molten rock from the mantle

mantle hot layer of Earth beneath the crust

marine organism plant or animal that lives in the ocean

metamorphic rock rock formed when igneous or sedimentary rocks are changed by heat or pressure

micrograph photograph taken through a microscope

mineral naturally occurring particle. Rocks are made from minerals.

molten melted

piezoelectricity ability to vibrate at a certain speed when an electric current is passed through

polymorph minerals that contain the same atoms, but have different atomic structures

rock cycle unending process of rock formation and destruction

sedimentary rock rock formed from the broken pieces of other rocks

stalactite thin icicle-shaped lump of rock that forms as water drips down from cave ceilings

stalagmite short, stubby column of rock that forms when water drips on to a cave floor and evaporates

synthetic crystal crystal made artificially

thin section very thin slice of rock mounted on a microscope slide

twinning when two crystals grow into or through one another

weathering breaking down of rock

INDEX